SELECT A STORY
Instant Ideas for Creative Writing

Grades 3–6

Written by Linda Schwartz
Illustrated by Beverly Armstrong

To the Teacher

Select-a-Story is a book of instant ideas for creative writing. It consists of thirty-seven instruction pages and a reproducible creative writing award. On each page is a story starter – a sentence, paragraph, or list designed to stimulate the reader's imagination and to define a writing challenge. For example, one page offers readers an opportunity to open and explore the space behind the doors to a clubhouse, a hotel, a locker room, a pet shop, a spaceship, and a test kitchen. Another page includes a list of thirty creatures – all of whom would be perfect characters in a truly monstrous tale.

Working alone, with a partner, or in small groups, students use these pages as the inspiration for creative writing assignments. First a student chooses an activity and reads it carefully. Then, he or she follows the instructions to create a story. Because the instructions are open-ended, the possibilities are bounded only by youthful imaginations.

As variations, you might suggest that students

- select two or more pages, and combine ideas from them to create a story;
- use characters and a plot they have already created but rewrite the story in a different form so that it becomes a fable, a fairy tale, a mystery, a news story, or a tall tale;
- convert a narrative story they have written into script form for production as a classroom drama, movie, or teleplay by adding stage directions and dialogue;
- change a dialogue they have written into a story by adding description and narrative;
- use a previously written story as the basis for a story board on which they illustrate the action – cartoon style – in a specified number of frames.

You'll find many uses for these activities in your classroom. Because their illustrations are whimsical and eye-catching, they are perfect for perking up a bulletin board or creating a decorative display. If you laminate them or slip them into clear plastic sleeves, they'll survive repeated handling as one much-used part of a busy creative writing center. They're ideal activities for students who finish everything quickly and effective incentives for students who find it difficult to finish projects. In short, these activities will help you get the most out of your eager writers and motivate your reluctant ones.

For additional doses of instant inspiration, purchase the companion book entitled **Pick a Picture.**

Copyright ©1989
The Learning Works, Inc.
Santa Barbara, California 93160
All rights reserved.
Printed in the United States of America.

Sixty-Second Spot

Write a text for a sixty-second radio commercial. To help you plan, listen to several radio ads. Notice what gimmicks are used to get your attention, how many times the product names are mentioned, what features are highlighted, and what slogans are used to help you remember the products. Because your commercial is intended for use on radio, you should create vivid, decriptive copy that will enable listeners to visualize the produce you are trying to sell. When you have finished writing your commercial, read it aloud and time your reading to be sure that it does not take more than sixty seconds.

Book Return

Many public libraries set aside one week each year for encouraging people to return overdue books. Write a humorous story about a library book that is **ten years** overdue. Describe the unusual circumstances that have prevented its return for so long a time.

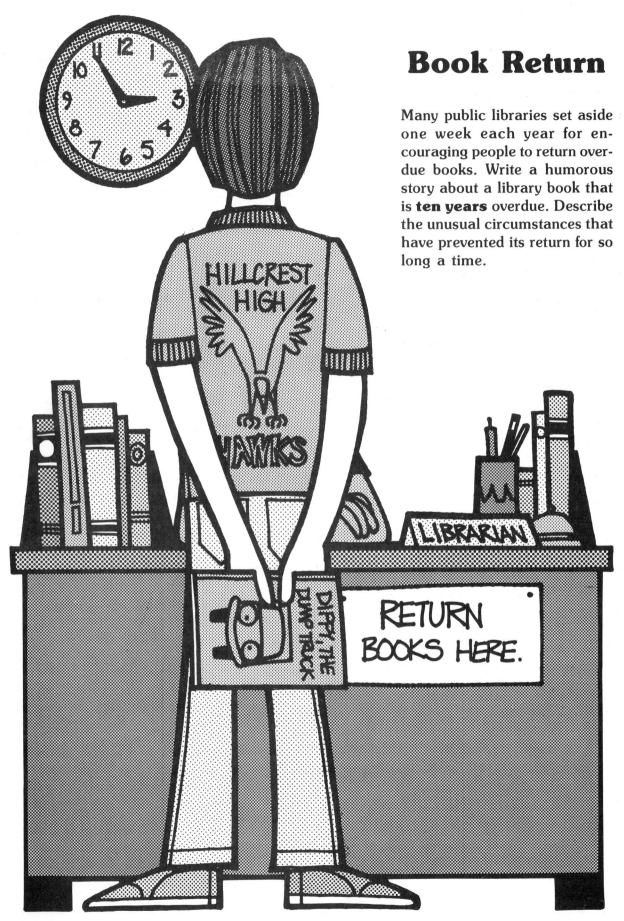

Explore a Door

Select one of the doors pictured below or create a door of your own. On a separate sheet of paper, draw a picture of the door you have selected or created. Cut around your door on the top, one side, and the bottom so that it can be opened. Swing the door open, and pretend that you are actually going through it. Write a short story about what happens behind the door. Mount your story and door side by side on a large sheet of paper. Display them where others can read and enjoy.

Chocolate Concoction

Suppose that you have been asked to create a special chocolate dessert in honor of National Chocolate Lovers' Week. What is the most mouth-watering dessert you can concoct using anything chocolate, including brownies, cake, candy, chocolate chips, fudge sauce, ice cream, and/or sprinkles? Draw a picture of your concoction on a separate sheet of paper. Below the picture, print the recipe for it or write an irresistible description of it.

The Blootz

You are the first person ever to see a Blootz! Write a description of this creature. Use colorful words to tell what a Blootz looks like, where it lives, what noises it makes, what it eats, how it defends itself, and how it cares for its young. Be sure to note all identifying marks, mention any striking features, and describe unusual behavior patterns.

Invention Convention

You have been invited to attend the Tenth Annual International Invention Convention. Other delegates have told convention organizers that they want to see you demonstrate the device you invented to make life easier. Write a detailed description of your invention in which you tell how you built it, what it is supposed to do, and how it works.

A Penny For Your Thoughts

Write a story about a penny. Select a title for your story from the list below or create one of your own.

Titles

Auntie Penny

Buried Treasure

The Case of the Copper Penny

The Coin Collection

Finders Keepers

The Lucky Penny

A One-Cent Sale

The One-Cent Swindle

Penny Auntie

The Penny Burglary

A Penny Saved

Penny Wise

Thrash Through the Trash

Pretend that your family purchased tickets in a lottery offering as first prize a fabulous trip for four to Walt Disney World. When the winning number is called, you know that it's yours; but you can't find the ticket anywhere. Where could you have put it? Write a humorous story about your family's frantic search for the winning lottery ticket. Describe all of the places you look and tell whether or not you eventually find it.

Hollywood Scene

Suppose that a Hollywood television producer has asked you to come up with ideas for a new situation comedy series featuring a family similar to your own. What would you call this new series? Whom would you cast to play each member of your family? Write a brief description of the first episode based on something humorous that actually happened to you and your family.

What's Up?

First, read this list of longer words that contain the two-letter word *up*. Next, see how many *up* words you can add to the list. Then, write a whimsical story in which you use at least fifteen of these words. (**Caution**: your story must make sense. It's not fair simply to list the words!) Finally, underline all of the *up* words that appear in your finished story.

up-and-coming	upon	upshot
up-and-down	upper	upside
up-and-up	uppercase	upside down
upbeat	upper class	upstage
upbraid	upper crust	upstairs
upbringing	uppercut	upstart
update	upper hand	upstate
upend	uppermost	upstream
upgrade	uppity	upstroke
upheaval	upraise	upswing
uphill	upright	uptake
uphold	uprising	uptight
upholster	uproar	up-to-date
upkeep	uproot	up-to-the-minute
upland	ups and downs	uptown
uplift	upscale	upturn
upmost	upset	upwind
	upshift	

A Legend in Your Own Time

A **legend** is a story that had its origins in the oral narratives of the past; is based on supposedly historical, though unproved, fact; and has been handed down within a culture from one generation to the next. The story of King Arthur is a legend, or group of legends. Arthur was king of England and leader of the Knights of the Round Table. He carried a special weapon, a sword with a jeweled hilt, which was called Excalibur. Derived from Latin, this name means "to free from the stone." One Arthurian legend tells how a magician named Merlin set this sword in stone and decreed that it could be removed only by a future king. As a young boy, Arthur was able to pull Excalibur from the stone and prove his right to the English throne. Write a story about the legendary hero King Arthur and about the magic powers of his sword, Excalibur.

Dollar Days

Did you ever wonder how many times a dollar bill changes hands? Pretend that you are a one-dollar bill hot off the press at the U.S. Bureau of Printing and Engraving in Washington, D.C. Write a detailed account of your first seven days in print. Describe your journey from hand to hand, purse to wallet. How do different people earn you? What do they use you to buy? What is it like to be in a pocket, a purse, a bank vault, a cash register drawer, or a bill-changing or vending machine?

A Sibling Fable

A **fable** is a short story in which human faults or weaknesses are described through the words and actions of animals. Although fables are usually amusing, their primary purpose is to teach a useful lesson, or **moral**. Suppose that your younger brother or sister is really "bugging" you. He or she won't listen to reason but may be willing to read an entertaining story. Write a fable that will teach him or her to respect your property and your privacy. Use animals as your main characters, and conclude with a sentence that summarizes the story and cleverly states the lesson you are trying to teach.

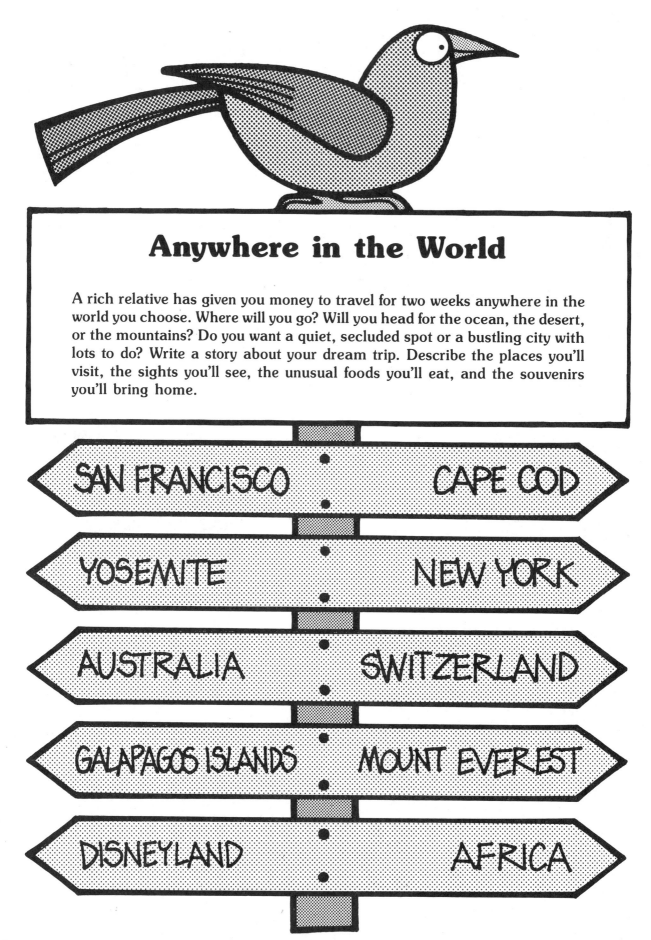

Anywhere in the World

A rich relative has given you money to travel for two weeks anywhere in the world you choose. Where will you go? Will you head for the ocean, the desert, or the mountains? Do you want a quiet, secluded spot or a bustling city with lots to do? Write a story about your dream trip. Describe the places you'll visit, the sights you'll see, the unusual foods you'll eat, and the souvenirs you'll bring home.

SAN FRANCISCO   CAPE COD

YOSEMITE   NEW YORK

AUSTRALIA   SWITZERLAND

GALAPAGOS ISLANDS   MOUNT EVEREST

DISNEYLAND   AFRICA

Plan
A Party

To earn extra spending money, you and a friend have started a party-planning business. Your first assignment is to plan a birthday party for twelve six-year-olds. First, decide on a theme for the party. Then, tell what this theme is and describe in detail how you will carry it out in the invitations, decorations, food, favors, games, and prizes.

Shaping the Future

First, look carefully at the futuristic shapes below, and let your imagination soar. Then, write a paragraph describing how one or more of these shapes might be used in the future in a home, on a playground, in an office building, in a vehicle, in a space station, or in any other place or object you can think of. Finally, draw a picture of what you have described.

Prized Possession

All of us own things we treasure. Some of these things are valuable because of what we paid for them or what someone else would pay to own them. Others are valuable because of the fun we had finding them, the people who made them for us or gave them to us, the occasions they commemorate, or the memories we associate with them. Of all the things you own, which possession do you prize most highly? Describe how you came to own this thing and tell why it is so important to you.

Glove Stories

First, select one of the pairs of gloves pictured below. Next, draw a larger picture of these gloves on a separate sheet of white art paper. Then, write a short story about the person who wears these gloves. Describe an exciting adventure he or or she had or something important he or she did. Finally, mount your finished story and glove drawing on a large sheet of paper so that it looks as if the story you wrote is being held by the gloves you drew.

auto racer's gloves

fire fighter's gloves

 **knight's gloves**

 **astronaut's gloves**

 **boxing gloves**

surgeon's gloves

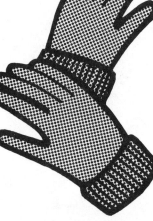 **skier's gloves**

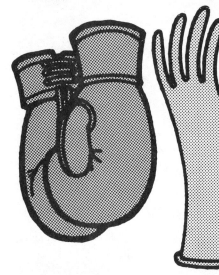 **gardener's gloves**

Once Upon a Time

A **fairy tale** is a short story about the adventures of fantastic beings, such as fairies, goblins, and wizards. Fairy tales often involve magic powers and may include the casting or breaking of spells. These stories usually begin with the phrase, "Once upon a time." Select one word from each of the four categories below. Write an original fairy tale that begins with "Once upon a time" and includes all four of the words you have selected.

Characters	Animals	Settings	Objects
dwarf	bear	beach	apple
elf	cat	bridge	beans
fairy	dog	castle	bell
genie	donkey	cave	caldron
gnome	dragon	cottage	candle
goblin	fox	dungeon	coach
little boy	frog	forest	glove
little girl	leopard	grotto	ladder
old man	lion	inn	lamp
old woman	rabbit	lake	pea
prince	rooster	meadow	potion
princess	sheep	road	pot of gold
troll	snake	tower	rainbow
witch	unicorn	town	ring
wizard	wolf	village	wand

Pick a Pet

For your birthday, you have received a gift certificate from the local Pick-a-Pet Shop. This shop stocks every kind of live creature a person might keep as a pet, including cats, chameleons, crickets, dogs, finches, gerbils, goldfish, hamsters, hermit crabs, parakeets, parrots, rabbits, snakes, tarantulas, tropical fish, turtles, and more. The shop also sells aquariums, cages, terrariums, food, vitamins, and all of the equipment needed to keep these creatures safe, comfortable, and healthy. The amount of your gift certificate is large enough to cover any pet you choose and all of the equipment you'll need to take good care of your pet for a year. Write a story in which you describe the pet you'll pick, and tell what other things you'll buy and why.

Life Shapers

Write an essay describing someone who has been influential in shaping your life and helping you become the person you are. This someone could be a parent, an aunt, an uncle, a grandparent, a friend, a teacher, or anyone else you have admired and learned from. Give specific examples of ways in which things this life shaper has said or done have affected you.

President for a Day

Every four years, adult citizens of the United States go to the polls to elect a new president. If you had the opportunity to become president, what could you do to make the world a better and a safer place? Describe several things you would do as president and tell how each one of these measures would help.

Conversations From the Past

Suppose that you were assigned to interview someone famous from the past and could spend an entire day talking with and learning from this man or woman. Whom would you interview? Choose one of the people listed below or someone else whose ideas and accomplishments interest you. First, list twenty questions you would ask. Then, write a paragraph describing what you hope to learn from the answers to these questions.

Famous Figures From the Past

Louisa May Alcott
Clara Barton
Ludwig van Beethoven
George Washington Carver
Charlie Chaplin
Samuel Clemens
Davy Crockett
Marie Curie
Charles Dickens
Emily Dickinson
Walt Disney
Amelia Earhart
Albert Einstein
Benjamin Franklin
Vincent van Gogh
Harry Houdini
Thomas Jefferson
Helen Keller
John F. Kennedy
Martin Luther King, Jr.
Abraham Lincoln
Golda Meir
Florence Nightingale
Annie Oakley
Georgia O'Keeffe
Pocahontas
Marco Polo
Jackie Robinson
Will Rogers
Eleanor Roosevelt
Betsy Ross
Sacagewea
William Shakespeare
Booker T. Washington

An Important Event

Our lives are made up of individual events. Some of these events are important, while others are insignificant. Write an essay about the most important event that has occurred in your life. Explain the circumstances that led up to this event, describe how the event affected you, and tell how it has changed your life.

It's a Mystery

A **mystery** is a piece of fiction about solving a crime, finding the answer to a puzzle, or explaining a mysterious disappearance. Write a story in which something mysterious occurs and someone solves the mystery by discovering who did it or how it happened. In creating your story, give careful thought to the following elements:

setting—where and when the story takes place

characters—the actors in the story; the people that the story is about

plot—the overall plan of the story; what happens when and to whom

action—what the characters do

motive—why the characters do it

solution—discovery or explanation of who did it and/or how it happened

Possible Titles

The Case of the Missing Mummy
The Clue in the Broken Clock
Hidden Doors and Secret Passages
The Howl of the Hound
Mystery at Midnight
A Noise in the Attic
The Poisoned Pen
The Purloined Locket
The Shadow

Personal Profiles

A **profile** is a brief biographical sketch, or word picture, of someone. Interview an adult whom you admire concerning his or her early years, education, career, and special interests. Ask the questions listed below or create your own. During the interview, take detailed notes. After the interview, use these notes to write a profile of the person you interviewed.

Early Years

1. Where were you born?
2. Do you have any brothers or sisters?
3. Did you have a pet as a child? If so, what kind?
4. What was your favorite toy?
5. Did you collect anything as a child? If so, what?
6. Who were your close friends while you were growing up?
7. What things did you and your family enjoy doing together?
8. What special memories do you have of your childhood?

Education and Career

1. Where did you go to school?
2. What was your favorite subject in school?
3. What person influenced your life the most?
4. How old were you when you started your career?
5. What made you choose your present vocation?
6. What special training and/or education is needed for your job?
7. Describe a typical day on your job.
8. What do you like most about your work?
9. What do you like least about your work?
10. What is the most exciting or gratifying thing that's happened to you on your job?

Special Interests

1. What hobbies and special interests do you enjoy in your spare time?
2. What is the best book you've ever read?
3. What is your favorite food?
4. What three words best describe you?
5. What is one thing you would like to change about yourself?
6. What is one thing you would do differently if you could start over?

Found a Peanut

Suppose that, on your way home from school, you found a peanut lying on the grass. Although this peanut looked ordinary enough when you picked it up, it definitely was not your average goober! In fact, it possessed incredible magic powers. Write a story about your adventures with the magic peanut.

Opinion Please

Write an essay about an issue that is controversial and has more than one side. First, select an issue that you feel strongly about. Use one of the issues listed below or think of one of your own. Next, begin your essay by defining the issue and describing both sides. Then, take a stand and express your opinions in a well-developed argument.

Issues

animal research
cheating
the death penalty
drinking
drug abuse
endangered wildlife
gun control
health care
the homeless
pollution
poverty
smoking
year-round school

Create a Mood

Select one of the settings named below or choose your own. Write a paragraph about this setting. Describe the sights, sounds, smells, tastes, and feel of this place. Use carefully chosen adjectives to create its mood.

Settings

an amusement park after closing

a beach at sunset

a classroom during final exams

a football stadium during the big game

a flower garden on a spring morning

a major league ball park during the World Series

a museum after hours

a tent during a thunderstorm

a theater on opening night

the woods after a snowfall

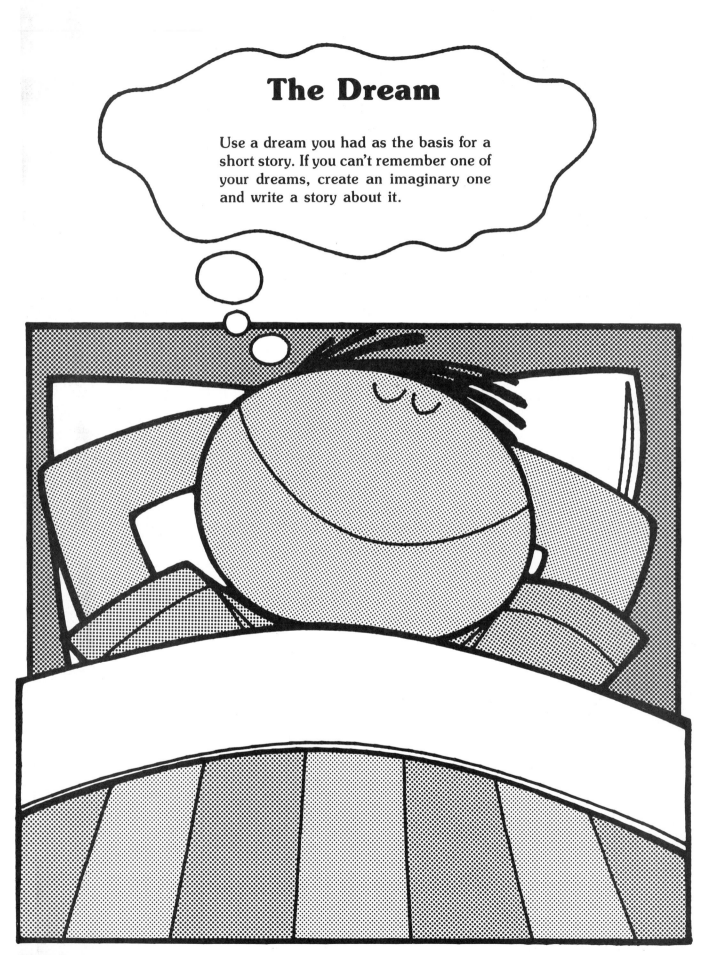

The Dream

Use a dream you had as the basis for a short story. If you can't remember one of your dreams, create an imaginary one and write a story about it.

Making Tracks

Trace the outline of your foot on a sheet of unlined paper. Within this outline, write about an interesting place your foot has been or something fun your foot has done.

Suggested Topics

climbing a mountain

dancing at a party

sliding into home plate

swimming in a pond or pool

ascending a long flight of stairs

standing still to watch a parade

kicking a winning soccer goal

walking across a beach

wading in an ocean

hiking in the woods

pedaling a bicycle

jumping off a pier

running a race

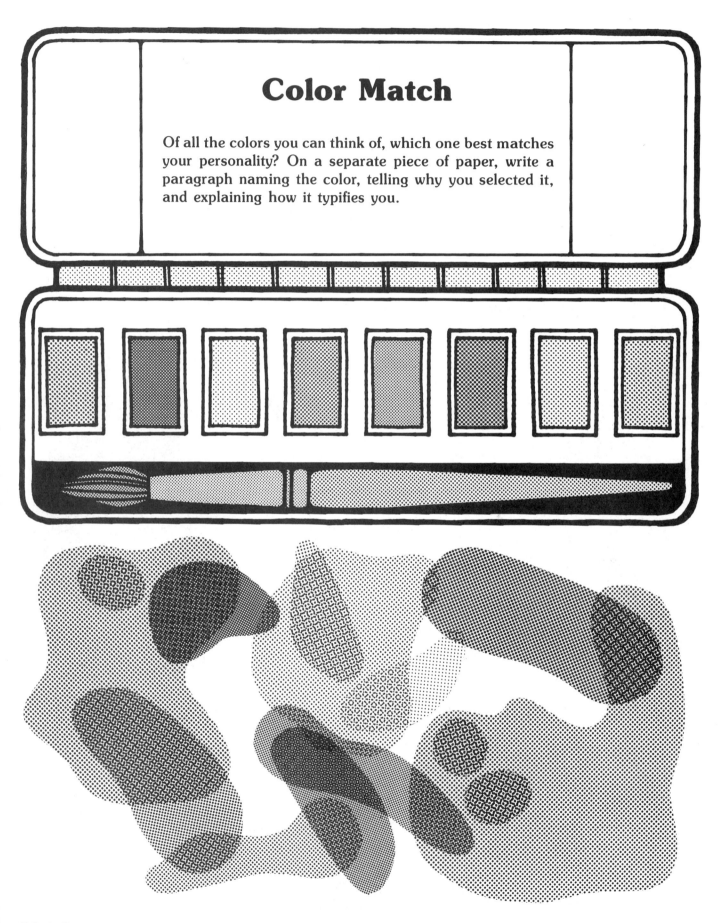

Color Match

Of all the colors you can think of, which one best matches your personality? On a separate piece of paper, write a paragraph naming the color, telling why you selected it, and explaining how it typifies you.

A Truly Monstrous Tale

First, use dictionaries, encyclopedias, or other reference books to find out something about each of the monstrous creatures listed below. Then, select one of these creatures and write a story about it. Use appropriate adjectives in vivid descriptions to create a truly monstrous tale.

Abominable Snowman
Argus
basilisk
Big Foot
centaur
Cerberus
Chimera
Cyclops
Dracula
dragon
Frankenstein's monster
gargoyle
Gorgon
griffin
Hydra
kraken
manticore
Medusa
Minotaur
Nessie (or Loch Ness monster)
phoenix
roc
Sasquatch
Sphinx
Titan
vampire
werewolf
wyvern
yeti

Pick a Proverb

A **proverb** is a brief saying that states a universal truth or expresses a choice morsel of folk wisdom. Pick one of the proverbs below, and write a short story using this proverb as the ending.

A bird in the hand is worth two in the bush.

A fool and his money are soon parted.

All that glitters is not gold.

An apple a day keeps the doctor away.

A rolling stone gathers no moss.

As the twig is bent, so grows the tree.

A stitch in time saves nine.

A watched pot never boils.

Be it ever so humble, there's no place like home.

Better late than never.

Do not count your chickens before they are hatched.

Do not cross that bridge until you come to it.

Don't cry over spilt milk.

Don't put all of your eggs in one basket.

Familiarity breeds contempt.

Grass does not grow on a busy corner.

Gratitude is the sign of noble souls.

Half a loaf is better than none.

Haste makes waste.

Honesty's the best policy.

If wishes were horses, beggars might ride.

It is easy to be brave from a safe distance.

Look before you leap.

Make hay while the sun shines.

Necessity is the mother of invention.

Never leave 'till tomorrow what you can do today.

Nothing is certain but death and taxes.

One bad apple spoils the bunch.

One picture is worth more than ten thousand words.

Only cowards insult dying majesty.

Outside show is a poor substitute for inner worth.

Pride goeth before a fall.

The grass is always greener on the other side of the fence.

The pen is mightier than the sword.

The way to a man's heart is through his stomach.

Variety is the spice of life.

You can't judge a book by its cover.

Twenty Feet Tall

Suppose that you woke up one morning and discovered, much to your dismay, you were 20 feet tall. Being this tall would be wonderful in many ways. You could easily see over crowds at parades and with just a few steps you could cover great distances. But on the other hand, things like bending down to tie your shoes or fitting in your bed would be quite difficult. Write a humorous story about a kid that was 20 feet tall for a day.

Fortunately / Unfortunately

Write a story in which the first sentence begins with the word *fortunately* and the next sentence begins with the word *unfortunately*. Repeat this pattern at least four times, but end on a fortunate note. Illustrate your story.

Example

Fortunately, I was walking home from a long day at school. Unfortunately, I stubbed my toe against an uneven place in the sidewalk and fell down. Fortunately, I happened to glimpse a crumpled dollar bill on the ground near where I landed. Unfortunately, a big gust of wind blew the bill away from my reaching fingers and down the street. Fortunately, I ran and caught the dollar bill before the wind blew it into a pond. Unfortunately, Big Bully Brewster was watching, and he grabbed it away from me. Fortunately, a passing police officer came to my aid and retrieved my dollar. Unfortunately, when I spent the dollar on a hot fudge sundae, I got a terrible stomachache. Fortunately, I recovered and am once again looking along the sidewalk for dollar bills others have accidentally dropped or carelessly overlooked.

Let's Talk

In its simplest form, a **dialogue** is a conversation between two people. Select any two of the people pictured below. Give these people names, and involve them in an interesting dialogue that reflects some of your own values and feelings. Write their dialogue in script form.

Example

TOM: (*resentfully*) No other kid my age has to look after his little sister. Why do I?

GRANDMOTHER: (*with understanding*) Few other kids your age have mothers who are concert pianists. When she practices or travels, she relies on me to care for you. I need you to help me keep an eye on Cindy.

Amazing Author Award

presented to

_____

by

_____

on this date

_____